DISCOVER SERIES
PLAYA

Spanish Edition

Pelota de Playa

Cubeta de Playa

Silla de Playa

Playa Cerrada

Bicicleta Crucero

Piedras de Playa

Toallas de Playa

Collar de Cuentas

Traje de Baño de Papá

Hamaca

Salvavidas Juvenil

Anillo de la Vida

Máscara y Snorkel

Mensaje en la Botella

Traje de Baño de la Mamá

Palmera

Castillo de Arena

Dolar de Arena

Colección de Conchas del Mar

Crema para el Sol

Gafas de Sol

Tablista

Aletas de Natación

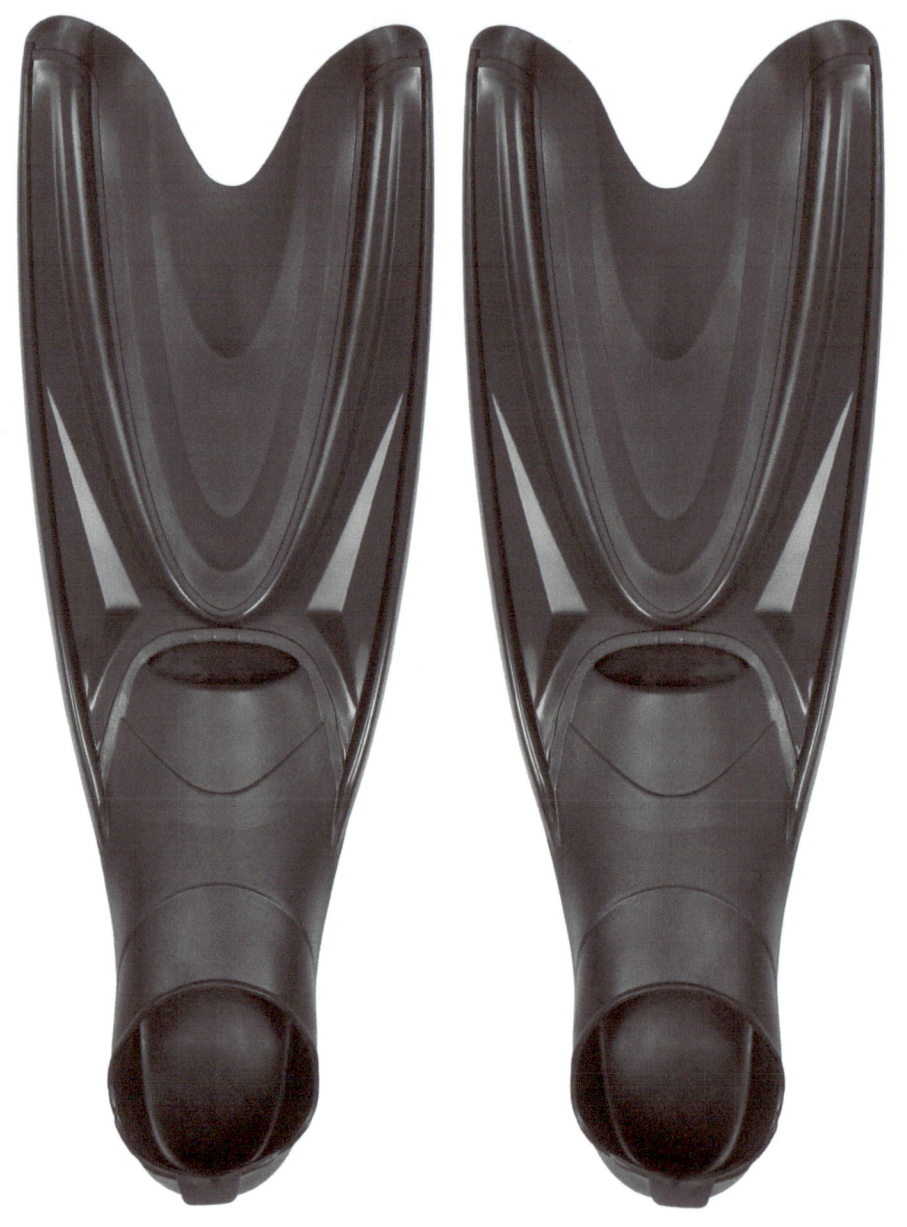

Anillo de Natación

Voleibol

Make Sure to Check Out the Other Discover Series Books from Xist Publishing:

Published in the United States by Xist Publishing
www.xistpublishing.com
PO Box 61593 Irvine, CA 92602

© 2017 First Bilingual Edition by Xist Publishing
Spanish Translation by Victor Santana
All rights reserved
No portion of this book may be reproduced without express permission of the publisher
All images licensed from Fotolia
ISBN: 978-1-53240-1-169 EISBN 978-1-53240-1-602

xist Publishing

www.ingramcontent.com/pod-product-compliance
Lightning Source LLC
LaVergne TN
LVHW071031070426
835507LV00002B/106